God's
Odd
Look

Gail
Fox

ISBN 0 88750 191 5 (hardcover)
ISBN 0 88750 192 3 (softcover)

Drawings by Margaret Hughes
Design by Michael Macklem

Printed in Canada
PUBLISHED IN CANADA BY OBERON PRESS

I

For Margaret

INVOCATION

Who's there?

I wish I knew

How to reach you
over mountains, continents,
histories, mythologies

Call your names, know your
many entries into space and your
returns

See the foresight, insight
of your many eyes, the double
bodies

But most of all, the
human heart of now and not
some other time

If you are anywhere

If you know my names

If you are there and
I am trying

If anything be true,
responsible, beautiful or
right

Let it be the answer to my
question

Let me stare me in the face

APPLES

Ah, the faces of the
dreamers here. . . .

So many Christs come to us
at Easter, Christmas,
and St. Valentine's Day. . . .

Last night I was stunned
by the secret smiles of
women on my ward. . . .

Perhaps they were in their
Gardens of Eden, the minds
so shut and perfect in their way. . . .

The bodies so disreputable,
stagger here and there—
but the faces. . .

Ah, it's ecstasy to
know what faces are. . . .

Conversions of disasters
into harmonious figs, apples,
friendly snakes. . . .

Listen, if you were a
face in here you would also
share this secret. . . .

Do not smile—it is
essential not to smile. . .

But laugh, they dream
such round and wondrous
apples. . . .

ABSOLUTES

If there is genius,
then it is everyone,
and not this pallid
suffering of the deities

bound to shoes and
shirts and second-hand
wings that cannot
elevate.

Lord, give me wings
that will get me up, and
if I crash, give me
the courage of spilled blood.

But do not make me
half-genius, half-idiot,
so that I cannot learn
Your absolutes.

CONVERSATION

There is no-one
here to discuss the
world with—

the raging tempests
of war and famine,
the indeterminate

millions dying daily
from lack of love
and head-on crashes

of the brightly painted
vehicles of passion–
there is no-one.

Who are these people
talking of lost
safety-pins

and girdles that reduce
their girths by inches,
while the

mad hatters pour
tea and serve magic
mushrooms

so that I am forced
to stumble as I
walk

to find my balance.
The power of the
tigers

keeps me from
talking of the real
world where my

every fantasy can be
enacted—in here,
the lesser kind of

evil that is an
effective plug to the
emotions.

I would rather talk
to someone of the
world situation

than of my problems—
sore throat, bad eyes,
and a body that

absorbs the pain of
others and suffers
periodically from the depression

of my loved ones.
So I write my spoken words,
I commune

with paper and hope
that someone will offer
to listen

today or tomorrow
or sometime before my
patience

runs out and I, out of
desperation, will have a
conversation

about the zipper on
my pants, which needs
to be replaced

or fitted with another
tongue to ensure safe
binding of the

wounds I close off
from everyone except
my notebook,

pencil and paper,
medium for my
lonely global energy.

ELEGY

For Pat Rieper

I am not destroyed
by ignorance—that's
life—but death does
destroy me

The young girl smashed
in an auto wreck
desperately trying to
hug her boyfriend

Unseen for weeks
while she lived in the
Mad House—quiet, demure
and blond as death—

She got it last night,
reincarnated into
something else: Spirit,
Devil, Mack the Knife.

It's not true. I'm
destroyed by ignorance
too. The half-hour of the
clock it took her

to leave the Mad House
for good—tough farewells—
and then the steering
wheel through the hip.

Life at its richest—
the grim Reaper of her
patronymic—I spin
in bewilderment.

CARTOONS

What the poor devil
thought she was doing in
that nightmare

drawing pictures on her
wrists, the artistic
razor

doing such weird
cartoons of her husband
lover–

Listen, Michael,
I talked to her for
a while

because the lump of
leaving you was
too real

I tried to tell
her, "Don't do such
things to your

beautiful wrists,"
and she knew she
shouldn't

Then she drew some
pencil sketches of
caterpillars

and horses and the
ideal woman with
a mare's

head running through
her face–Michael,
it was too late

for romance and
I left her almost
sobbing with

relief that she
had found me to
talk to

While I came
here to this half-lighted
room of

snoring loonies to
draw this poem
across the wrist

of my last touch
of your beautiful
hand

Do you know I
am an artist with
words?

That I want to
fuck the dictionary
or go blind

so that I can
forget the way things
look here

and only describe
them with symbols and
sounds?

That poor devil
with her talented
razor and eyes

looking everywhere
for the blood
under the bandages

And then me with
my black pen
writing

these idiotic
poems—what is
the sanity

that I find with
these crazy words
together

impossible symbols
to recommend your
whole beauty to me

The time of weeping,
the time of dying,
the time of sleep

draws near—Michael,
I crawl from here
to a

very dark bedroom
without you, but
clutching this poem

about my life—
is that a kind of
slashing of the

wrists? Already
my hot blood rises,
Michael.

MUSIC

The criminal in me
longs to break the piano,
to Beethoven,

While the television,
in its frenzy, saps
the energy of these

creative people,
drugged and comatose,
trailing smoke.

Not break, but play
so simply and freely that
this Karmic Wheel

which brought them
to their feet, breaks
to my music,

and we are all
reborn and resurrected
as gods.

The criminal in me
longs to play such beautiful
music that

We are all oblivious
to the television and what
it whispers—

Ah, the crashing
chords about my head,
the assault of senses!

The ecstasy with
edges, the controlled
drunkenness!

NIGHT

The night of
calamity has descended,
when stars

'flabbergast the
world with spots of
light no bigger

than my fingers,
when great thoughts
are spoken between

lovers, and a
vast certainty of
darkness

cradles our fingers
that long to
twist everything.

Then my love, I
sit in my chamber
of the damned

and write such
poems the world has
never seen,

as night and savage
hearts quicken when
I decide

to return to the
Eden of the
absolute creation

and direct my
energy to affairs
of Hecate

who rules the
night, and clamours
for a fierce being

to hold up sky and
earth upon a single
muscle

so that when the
sun awakens, we will
be free of

night's vision, and
I will rest, me,
the axis of the universe.

THE VAN GOGH BEDROOM

She loved her. Not
strongly like a piece of chocolate,
but steadily. From
day to day. Gulp and
release of breath. Do I love you?
The mirror, steady as an
eye. The answer, self-evident.

Have some Dutch
chocolate. Thanks. The
dark variety with nuts. She bit.
The sugar swept through
her teeth, numbing her blood
and brain. She would come later.

Breathless. An artistic
mop of hair. She understood the
reasons for the chocolate. But
not for her. Do I love you?
The answer, self-evident.

A picture of people, eating.
Not chocolate, but
potatoes. They have their ways.
She had the chocolate.
The bedroom, swirling.

Though not an artist,
she would come. Breathless.
Numbing her blood and
brain. You are more beautiful

since I have brought you
chocolate. Was she dreaming?
The single steady eye.

A picture of a cypress. The
room swirling, the windows
closing with the dark. Trees
are so beautiful when
painted. Gulp and release of
breath.

Have another chocolate.
Thanks. The dark variety with
hazel nuts. She bites. An
inner warmth, more than
happiness. The vibrations of the
cypress eat the light. A
warmth. She loved her.

She loved her from day
to day. Steadily, like the
mirror. The potato-eaters,
eating. The cypress, gulping
light. She was the
dark artist in the mirror.
Do I love you?

Swirling, everything. The
chocolate sliding down her
throat. An Alp, a precipice.
And then? She loved her.
Gulp and release of breath.
The mirror, watching. The
answer, self-evident.

QUEST

Carrying the crutch
of cigarette butt between
my fingers

I perambulate the
strange and twisting
corridor

It's straight, they
tell me

No, I find it
labyrinthine because I
must decide

whether I will
find the fabled minotaur

or stay in here forever

And if I stay whether
I will be schizophrenic
as they tell me

or irrevocably sane
and ugly

For there is an ugliness
to their Weltanschauung

I despise the grey
tapestries of their
desires

If I seek the minotaur
and find him I will die or
worse

I will drink from their
fountain to give me life

I could not stand such
contentment

Perhaps I'll give up
and return to Medea and her
magic

Drowse in her arms and
dream I've found the fleece

THE IMPOSSIBLE

The impossible seeks
a body, a vehicle
to prove itself,

a pristine vase,
an artefact that the
oceans

have covered up.
The impossible is
with us, but in

another form of
energy, driving men
to genius

or insanity. This
time, this grief
of civilization is

granted more
impossibility than
ever.

Why, my people,
do we ignore our
gifts,

and pledge each
other not to drink
or eat

the vehicle of the
impossible, the imagination
which is lust,

the turncoat
soldier, who with
wounded arm

and leg, gives in
to the enemy and
finds himself?

The impossible
rules us, the impossible
causes us to think

feelings of omnipotence,
procedures of
great merit

which the world
may recognize or the
world will

scorn, but which
never will lodge in the
forgotten lobe

of the brain. My people,
we are ambidextrous,
we are impossible

in what we know.
Let us pray to our
Father,

upon whom the
bane of creation
rests,

and cherish each
venture into the
unknown.

For those who
would have the
impossible,

for those who would
know the sanity
in death,

for those .brave
psychic mariners,
there is a kind of

health reserved
for the very gifted
and the very pure

in heart. A glimpse
of eternity, and
God's holy chariot,

speeding them to
rest in his
Nothingness.

JOB (22 APRIL)

Job–you are the
perfect metaphor for
what I am–

the ache and boil
of my inside out,
while my outside in

speaks with
tongues of honey and
fruit of figs

and wanders disconsolate
around the wreck
of humans

that stagger somewhat
differently from me
about

their circles, more
like jelly than me, the
hard centre

vibrating the load
of dynamite, and I
the Job

that cannot help
but see the job to
do

but cannot speak
of this to anyone
I know. . . .

The walls shake
with disaster while
I hang on

to my bed, rolling
through my dreams
hard-headed

trailed by comforters
bringing milk and
other welcomes

And God (who is that?)
tests me with the
hardest thing

my love, my feelings
of inadequacy for
those who love me

or don't; and if you
don't, please
speak

I cannot bear the
silence of your rich
senses

but worse, I cannot
endure not knowing
what you are

how you are, what
you mean by this attempt
to love my shadow

love my idea of
me—listen, I will not
suffer for nothing!

if I knew you
were not waiting somewhere
there

in the centre of
my palm, a heart that
speaks of silence

and love to be gained
through saying nothing
but praise, amen. . . .

If these are vain
words and should not
be uttered

if my steadfast
prayer for help will
not be met

then I succumb
to my comforters and bid
them entrance

But if you are
aware of my circumstance,
if you know

my heart, then
take it back to your
hand

and give it love,
and think of it
nights

when we are not
together, when our
lives are torn apart

and we drift further
from each other
like arks

upon two separate
floods of life. . . .
Angry gods!

There is but one
God, I will listen
only to him

and if you comfort
me with quiet longing,
I will not quit.

WORDS OF LIFE

"...if words are breath,
and breath is life..."
—Hamlet

How do we dance
our music true
when our minds fight
the rhythms that our
bodies construe?

How do we write
our poetry breathing
when words are breath
and none of us know
meaning?

How do we play
our instruments whole
when the negative
beat assumes the
heart's role?

It is the forgotten
desire we must
resurrect—the cracked
emotions, situations,
broken fists.

Must connect them
living and dancing to our
songs, so that when we
love, they connect us
to ourselves.

DARKNESS

For Stancy

There is nothing awkward
about darkness.

Dark sky into earth
and the warm breath of all these
dark, complicated people,
flowing light.

At the beginning, my
muscles were so struck by light,
I couldn't stretch.

It took the acceptance
of great darkness within my body
to show me the shadows
beyond the body—that small wing
contracting in the light edges
of the shadows, wanting nothing
but total sunstroke.

But now it is so right,
so necessary to surrender to this
rich, unknowable world without
horizon.

To stand with out-stretched
hands, not wanting to ask
whether they are reaching
in the same direction.

Or whether what they touch
is day or night.

WORKSHOP

In this workshop,
we learn to build

Birdhouses with
holes too large for birds

Too small for humans

Holes we cannot squeeze
through

That birds cannot plug
with straw

Holes that are energy
leaks, claptrap visions of the
world

The world being these
houses, ready to explode

God give us houses of
sanity

Or let us be, God,
wholly what we are

Personally, God, your
dreams that made us are
Frankenstein

Or was it us, God,
who made these bird-houses,
these holes

Of infinite awkwardness,
wobbling like cripples in the
broken air

Chips fly like dynamite
Someone is building a monstrosity

Let him build, Lord,
and help us all

With the houses of
our insanity

With the houses of
our love and terrible calm

RAIN

It rains today

The slick wet slides
through the air

Like Nefertiti's
smile under the crown of hair

She was so beautiful
I suppose I knew her once

Now the rain reminds me
that I must learn to weep

For those beautiful
ones who changed the world

Those political lovers

Whose very face was
enough to

Burn down the ships of
Ilium and

Write great poems of
blood across the walls

Their writing, their
cuneiforms of conquest

Rain is so necessary
upon the stones of Pompeii

Lovers, beautiful ones
haunt me

In the rain of the
ancient world

STONE SPIRITS

Stones matter little

They break into hundreds
of pebbles

Stonehenge disintegrates
and chalk, the rock of
writing, scatters

We are breaking, too

The politicians tell us
nothing of our spirit

It hangs in the air
like a great noose around
our necks

We are not stones
yet, but soon

Soon we will die upon
the tree of life

But that too is
breaking

Every thing is like
stone eventually

Although some of us
die sooner

And walk the streets
with the mad stride of a
warrior

Who knows without any
doubt

He must kill before he
eats his supper

Ah stones matter
little, and pebbles

But we are nothing
if we do not fight our
stony exteriors

And hang in our *rigor
mortis* screaming

For the last drink of
hemlock, the last
cigarette which does not
kill us

Rather the stones of
which earth has several

Stone eyes, stone
hearts, stone pyramids
where we are buried

Let us watch the sun
go down, it burns into
stony blackness

And then we know what
we are

Fathers against sons,
but bound with stones
ever after

THE BEAUTIFUL

The beautiful are like
children

They rock securely
as if mother were
somewhere near

As if anything they
did would be excused
because of their beauty

I do not speak of
body's beauty

I speak of the warm
glow of feeling

These beautiful reflect
into the mirror

Which is all of us
tied to our suffering

But their great
divinity shines through
their pain

And I cannot help but
smile at what I am

That woman with three
teeth, that man with
no hair

I think them beautiful
I must be mad to think at all

Instead I close my
eyes and the mirror
gives me what I want

The spirit in the
black-white karate belt
of conquest of my

Body's ugliness   Is
that not a foolish thing
to say

I am a fool about the
beautiful

Let it be ever this
way, O wise mirror

Seen through the
third eye which cannot
be proven

But which knows the
beauty of which I speak

The round apples of
the feelings

Offered freely as a
gift

CHESS

Chess is for men
who seem to care

that soldiers leave
their horses upside down,

when the battle gives
them nothing more to say

than blood and gore
and calamity. Angels

who speak of talismans
in the dark, and feed

their hungry poems to
poets who love angels

but cannot fuck,
do not know the wry

sophisticated graces
of the heart, and

cannot give advice
to those marvellous knights

who joust across the
tables of the soul with

perfect remedies for
conquest. Dear heart, I

write this exquisitely sad
and grieving game of chess

for you who don't know
the first thing about any game

God played, but love,
and even love was made to

get up and clunk away.
My mate, my denizen of night,

check me with your
beautiful sword and whip.

ABSENCE

What does love?

The quick intake of
breath when I

See you coming across
the head

A steady stream of
traffic and then

Your face
glowing with incredible light

I can't believe that
you could be so beautiful

You must
give your heart to me

So I will not
out of loneliness

Call you anything
but God

Still, I could only
lie with what you

Represent and I could
not lie with God

What is love if not
this tender accident

And feeling you
with my rich senses

Which threaten the
ice of without you

If this is love
then you are its instrument

And you are God
after all

If you are not, I
love you anyway

Take me for what
I have just said

These are words of
bittersweet

Mind-fucking is a
lonely thing

You are probably
not with me as I write

Perhaps we should
promise that

On certain days we
think of each other

And picture and create
each other's flesh

Otherwise it is an
empty pleasure

But it's better
than fucking elephants

So be patient
with my terrible impatience

I'll come to you
yet. Yes.

II

DANCER

I

You danced for us
in the terror of darkness,
I said: "We need a dancer,
someone who will dance the War."

And you appeared,
wearing a large gold cross,
and the crowd went pale
with shock.

They picked you
out of the snow, they never
found the horses, or the
Russian sleigh you abandoned
when your brother fell to
madness.

But they did find you,
in the snow behind the
village, gathered you up,
a miracle, the final dance,
the summing up of your
intelligence, which leapt
around us like an animal we
felt obliged to watch.

A beast of movement, yet
drawn to contemplation of
dying soldiers and
concentration camps, those
blobs of blood and stale
excrement which at the
end prevented you from love.

Your only words were, finally,
"Can he jump?" pointing
to the powerless skeleton
of your flesh.

How tragic to call you
"Dieu de la Danse."

The Parisian critic
must have known that gods
are the solitary ones.

You bounded away on your
small silk slippers,
your half-closed slanting
eyes staring like some
kind of idiot.

The shopkeeper who
refused to sell you bread
didn't know that gods
need nourishment as well as
men, nor did he understand
your broken attempts to
speak the language, and
led you out to the streets.

"I am God," you wrote,
"we are the same." Your
eyes, totally empty of the
universe.

There was, of course,
a command performance–
Diaghilev.

And given the kind of
impresario he was,
what chance did you have?

For five years you
enacted the most demanding
roles, the Slave in
Scheherazade, the Spectre
of the Rose,

those shadowy beings,
half-man, half-woman, who
haunt our dreams.

"Not a robust dancer,"
someone said, "though not
effeminate."

On tours, your sister's
jealous rage when
prevented from sharing
your room, must have caused
you sorrow.

She wanted to enter your
closed and glittering
world, but there was no
room on the crowded stage
that was your bed.

4

The War, the War,
almost as if the
atrocities were planned
by God himself.

For who could
imagine tanks against a
horseback army,
barbed wire, poison gas?

Not God, you would say,
God is love, God is the
spirit of joy.

But where does the
suffering come from,
Nijinski?

For you have danced the
War and lost more than
people who live an entire
lifetime with their
minds intact.

They took a picture
then—your face thick as a
Cossack cap and shadows
around your eyes, wheeling
like birds of death.

Another war was over
and men had bullet-holes
in legs that used to dance.

Once you tried to
find a system of notating
human movement, and sat
at the piano with Stravinsky,
Diaghilev somewhere close.

The critics called you
mad, but were you?

The world was going to
war and people whispered
that in spite of that, you
saw God everywhere.

Then your wife returned
from the famous psychiatrist,
unable to speak.

"Femmka," you said, "you
are bringing me my death
warrant."

5

Before the War, you
danced *Scheherazade*, and
we who live too recently,
too brutally, forget the
way you danced,

the single *elevation*
that carried you across the
stage as if you were
possessed by God or
total weightlessness.

And when you danced,
they say, you almost reached
the heights of what we are,
and God became the fire
in the head, the earthquake
beating out the dance.

The bronze Negro
crouches for the leap, the
stage set shivers, the
lights dim to focus on your
face.

But we are the children
of the War and cannot watch
the dancers dance anything
but war.

Where are you, Nijinski,
and your feet built like
bones of birds?

"Everything is not horror,"
you wrote, "but joy."

Once the tumult was so great
that Diaghilev shouted:
"Silence! The dancers cannot
hear the music!"

The music stopped.

You returned to the
terror of the darkness.
"I will dance the War,"
you said.

THE VILLAGE IDIOT

1

whatever this
means

that I've
come here with
delusions and rage

that my nightmares
showed me an
idiot woman

that my left ear and
right nostril
cannot comprehend

may the idiot woman
show me sanity

may the idiot woman
hulk out in her
brown sweater

and take my thoughts
as she would
take herself

and rub until a
faint pleasure
burns

and breaks
like a night of
fireworks

2

and yet
after the first
shocking sight of her

I knew that
sanity was not the
blessing I had thought

and springs
not from the head's
lobotomy, but the heart's

and yet

to turn the
eye in any direction
was to discover

not total dark

but a chiaroscuro
that only the
idiot woman knows about

3

I'll sketch her
ruddiness, drool,
foul breath, hair,
glazed eyes, nose that
flares like a wet skirt

when I have her
down, just right,
I'll begin to see the
occasional sun, the
cowshit in the brain
when I try to think

but not until
I have included the
round shoulders, stubby
legs, slight hump of the
back

4

not unlike an
animal in a lab, haywire
with the shock of
breathing

she gets rabid,
grabs fistfuls of hair,
snake-dances from one leg to
what appears to be another

like a crowd around an
accident, my thoughts
gather

5

dragging for her
in the stream, the

village scooped the
skirts and somewhat
later

hauled her safe
with such ferocity
she

puked slime, scum,
weeds, slightly
heaving

after a change of
clothes, stood on the
street again

chewing her
cheeks, hands down her
skirts

(or so they told me)

6

despite certain
catastrophes

she never
collides with cars,
caterwauls

a matter of
timing, perhaps, or
breeding

but breeding so
suffocating that
genitals, guts, chunks of
brain atrophy

still, she has
some wretched secrets

love (something
unbearable) speaks
through me, furious

7

she walks, she
stumbles over fields,
lurches onto highways,
startled

loses her way,
giggles, rubs her
hands together

the pig cart comes
(the pig, newly killed
for Christmas)

she huddles inside,
locked up, pulled back
to the village

absurd the village,
and the pretensions
I have to understanding

when they killed the
pig, blood swept the stones
like twenty centuries

(she wore a
blood-red sweater)

I crouched like a
beast, unable to
articulate

(she wore the
same black peasant
skirts)

world of savages
what is it

9

thinking god-awful
of this and that

(the hair's breadth
between the rage and the
gobbledegook)

I saw her
outlined against the
terrible water

faces at the
windows uttering
words of prayer

let her drown,
they muttered

10

NO
not in the
pig-blood puddles

not where she
should be

heart pounding,
I search the landscape
for the answer to

this stage-fright,
lovesick,
state of mourning

nights, the
tossing of a branch
on the window

the restless
circling of the
moonlight

reminds me I'm
bewildered, can only
recall

her fierce
struggle with her
eyes

to keep them open
long enough for
whatever

register that
disturbance, then
succumb to the

uncertainty,
ridiculous half-light,
dull fever

finding her,
bringing her back

pork lips lobbing
spittle, slack-jaw to
forehead

stumbling through
half-witted bestial
flesh

does she have the
idiot face I've
imagined

or something
nonsensical, impossible
as death

this face in my
nightmares

that swims to
meet me in the mirror's
dark

BODY AND VILLAGE

"sick with desire and fastened to a dying animal"
—Yeats

I

The first thing
is to speak.

To let the new
tongue grow until it
makes the words as
easily as a curse.

But the first tongue
fights. Will not
relinquish its place.

The mouth grows sore
with argument.

In the meantime,
describe the village
without staring too
much.

But the eyes must
stare: the village
idiot.

Her tongue blathers
around her lips. The
new tongue makes similar
mistakes.

The mouth grows
sore. The mouth cannot
smile nor speak.

The two tongues wag
like villagers, leaning
out windows, asking
where you come from.

Foreigner, freak,
you must cut the first
tongue out.

There are dangers
in a double speech.

The village waits.

2

The body is
not the village.

It wants to become
like villagers who stare at
you–but can't.

Walking is an exhibition.

The arms swing in a
peculiar rhythm, not
yours.

The shoulders
stumble and stoop.

The body controls
what you do, but the
body is not you.

You must find out
what the body is, what
you're left with.

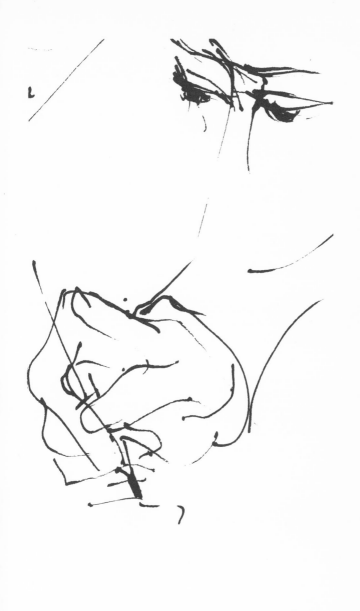

3

The head presents
itself uncovered, cold
(for now it's winter),
coughing slightly.

The village is
red-cheeked and curious
about the head.

You explain its
point of view, you say
everything you can,
but the words don't
come.

The head fills up
with gas (last night,
sauerkraut).

You cough, you
blow the nose, wipe the
eyes.

The head gives up.

4

The hand is a
problem.

It wants to shake the
village's hand, but the
village holds back.

The hand sulks,
hides in a pocket,
sticks holes in gloves.

You must
discipline the hand.

The village talks.

5

The ears pretend to
hear the words.
Ja, ja, always agreeing.

But sometimes the
ears *hear* the words.

The ears cannot
believe the village
would say such things.

The ears redden,
crawl into corners of the
head.

You must ask the
ears what was said.

6

You seize the
eyes and pluck them
out.

They hang from the
fingers like chicken
necks.

You imagine the
village in little pools of
blood, the future a
tiny thing, the people,
specks.

But the eyes ache. The
eyes see more than they can
hold.

Beyond this street
is another street.

The eyes will never
see the village whole.

7

The last thing
is to dream.

To imagine a
village where the
body has a place.

But tongue, head,
hand, ears cannot
accept, and run.

Suddenly, only you
are there, and the
idiot, looking for
words.

You have no
tongue. You have
neither legs nor feet.

You can only be
just there. With the
idiot. In the dream.

Faceless to the
village when you
awake.

CONVERSATION WITH MYSELF

For M

I am poet and
have need of wisdom

I am woman and
have need of man

Or woman or child
who can teach me the
essence of what I am

I am open,
but through my eyes
the light is vanishing

I am ready,
but it is almost winter,
leaves breaking and thundering
to earth

I have received a
vision of wholeness,
and abandon the search
for the holy act,
the ultimate meaning

I have received a
vision of wisdom and
choose that

Once it was happiness,
later, goodness–
the saint in me longed to be–

Now I search all
degrees of the circle,
all signs of the Zodiac

Self, I am open and
ready: speak

*Poet and woman,
do you know your body?*

*Do you know the
flow of electrons
through your hands?*

*Do you know what
it is to be human?*

*Do you know how to
laugh?*

*Have you considered
the passing of each
moment?*

*The vanishing of afternoon
into darkness
and the brave attempts
to stay awake?*

Have you thought
long and hard on the
meaning of cauliflower?

Have you danced
carelessly and slightly
drunk?

Do you know the
interface between mind
and feelings?

Have you wept
at the hunger of a sparrow
and seen divinity in a stone?

Do you believe
in the rights of criminals?

Can you control the
planetary wars, the famines
in your mind?

Do you want the insanity
which is part of you
to have the final word?

Or could you prefer
the ordinary to the extraordinary?

Can you endure the
language of the heart?

Poet and woman,
wisdom is a vision of the
soul at rest

Know that as you grow,
you amass the centuries,
and can choose their
wisdom or their ignorance

I choose wisdom, Self
but I have fears about
the path

You ask so much of me,
I tremble

Still my discontent
burns through me, my
senseless acts

I want the knowledge
of thin air and the
experience of drowning

Do I risk my soul
by asking?

Does Mephistopheles
dance behind my head?

Will my vision detach
me from the earth and
force me into celibacy?

My fear is real, I
light a cigarette

And turn on the
lights so I will not
be in darkness with this
fear of you, Self

Poet and woman,
do not force the fear
away

Let it flow through you
and define you

I sense your courage
although you know it
less than the taking
of a breath

Are you ready,
poet and woman?

I am

Then who are you?

I am the poet,
Gail Fox

And sometimes I am
woman and sometimes man

And sometimes I am
confused and often sad

What else?

I live a life of
outer chaos, but inwardly
there is discipline

How do you know?

I feel language
steady me and brace me
against the assault
of senses

Are you happy?

I am not happy now,
I am neutral, letting the
words flow through me
like a steel rod

A release of energy,
a breaking of resistance

Minds are neutral
territories and do not
know the sexual games we
play until too late

And then?

The heart which is the
only perfectable
instrument we have

Goes berserk and impedes
the growth of the spirit
in which we live

You mean we die

I mean the pressure
in us to become a well-read
book exerts until

We crack and memorize
each word, each cliché
of that slim volume

While the breath becomes
short and inadequate

To our needs, which are
to expand to our full
capacity

Every cell engaged,

Every act a fresh and
original occasion to
rejoice and suffer into

Knowledge of what we are

Breathing so slowly
that our life continues
until death

A living sustenance
to our hopes

A health unrestricted
by medicines that
conquer depression

Or elevation into space
where feet do not
touch ground

Or feel the gravity
of planet Earth

Poet and woman,
you are speaking of
yourself

Be more specific

Tell of your past

I was born a child
into a world I couldn't
understand

For those ancestors
talked in a fusion of
language and nerves

I was ill-equipped to
bear the strain of many
days alone

Aching to communicate
with strangers with whom
I shared a home

Those gentle people I
wanted so desperately to love

And even now it is a
tragedy to find I cannot
speak to these people and
be understood

For they inhabit a land
I forsake to allow
myself the privacy of
hope, dreams and
astral methods of escape

Leave, I told myself,
and I could not return

My soul floated above
my body but could not
connect to that flesh

That became the only
identity that made them mine

I began as a talker,
but gradually the silence
became a wall to pound
against

Year after year,
growing older and more
rebellious

In my attitudes and
failure to adjust to a
strict but gentle version
of a world in which I was
a total stranger and still am

*Poet and woman,
you are sad*

It makes me sad to speak
of these dear people

For they were important
for the wrong things
I did

And the reason that was
my glory, snapped

And I broke my body on
drink

While my people
stood by in rejection
and wordless agony

Watching me master
my failures with every
cell I had

Determined to be
completely opposite of
what they meant

And what they mean is a
loss of history

A hiatus in time
that prevents the easy
flow of friendship

And I weep for there is
an onion in my heart

A white vegetable of
passive power

That would make a
meal of my regrets and
accept them as they are

Persons with whom I
share a certain attitude

A certain type of blood

And, if all else fails,
a common heritage and
place of birth

O America! O my parents!

The blood so thick and
yet, the clots, the
blockages, the heart
attacks, the nerves

Revved to higher
and more sophisticated
methods of detecting

Truth, and rooting
it out

Self, I have discovered
a blind spot

Help me conquer the
bitterness
in my heart

Poet and woman,
freedom from the past
exacts a price

Reality tests the
best in us but

Suffering must be
positive

The price of that
freedom is honest loss

And when there can be
no other choice

The spectre of the past
catches us in our
solitude

At the height of our
powers, at the peak of
our achievement

Self, I am angry

Poet and woman,
the anger must leave
you

You are not a child

No longer do you seek
a mother in every woman
you meet

Allow the onion
to be cooked so the
heart will heal into
perfection

Self, there is
sensitivity in these
people

There is imagination
and an ordinariness I envy

For in my growing I
became an aristocrat

How could I have been
their child?

My snobbery
is basic to my needs

Is it, poet and woman,
or do you lie?

I lie, but that is
a defence to hide my
ignorance of a

Man with no education,
of a woman who does not
know Beethoven

To treat all as my
equal would be a necessity

To establish wisdom
in my heart

For it is not wisdom
of the mind I seek
with greater and greater
facts to flourish

But the language of a
human being connected
to love

*Those people, those
ghosts of the past
are your present*

*Clocks are a human
machine, but human
time cannot be measured*

*For memory renders
past as acute as present
pain*

*Poet and woman,
leave you parents,
tell more about your past*

What did you do?

I travelled into
inner space, into symbols
myth and dream

I spoke out loud
and discovered the power
of sound

I whispered symphonies
in my head and
learned of music

The counterpoint and
elegance of Bach

The majesty of Beethoven

The eloquence of Chopin

*Did you share these
experiences, talk of
them to others, check
that you were whole?*

No, I possessed them
for myself and was
strangely unaware

Of the world of people,
of feelings and the
precision of bodies

I learned the accuracy
of approximations and
excelled at theory

But I was clumsy,
and my body was not
part of me

Falling down in the
élévation, my dancing
teacher, irate and
bewildered

It was all wrong,
my lips rigid in their
smile

My classmates found me
eccentric with a
strange sense of humour

I laughed when I
should have cried

What did you study?

I applied myself to
music and mirrored its
nuances through every
mood-swing

Unpredictable, unsteady,
my hair grew long,
black turtlenecks, sandals
in winter

Esoteric jokes and lines
from poems that I had
memorized

Outwardly bold and
confident, but inwardly,
a mass of nerves

When my English
professor committed
suicide, for the first
time in my life, I
attempted to die

Did you recover?

I became more furious,
more extreme and cut off

My friends lost patience
and would have no part
of me

Alone, I began to write

Was it good?

It was a series of
screams from the neglected
heart

An attempt to explain
myself to others

And some began to
understand my fury and my
delicate state of balance

Like the poet, Robert Bly,
who wrote me: your poetry
is weird, but strangely
beautiful

I clutched his letter
to me in the dark

*What do you make
of this period of your
life?*

I see it as an
intense experiencing
of the negative

An allowing of myself
to know all evil and
call it, for want of a
better word, my goddess

Sarcastic, petulant,
I married a man who
would take care of me

And join with me
against the past

On the day of my wedding
I told myself:

You do this to destroy
yourself

And I went dead and
vegetable in my grief

You chose your life,
you made it what it was

Do you regret, do you
see these years as
waste?

I regret none of it,
although for years, I
suffered with my betrayal

And could not make this
suffering positive

We have talked of the
past, let us talk of
now

How did you get in
touch with me?

I chose to go mad,
thinking right or wrong,
that I would learn
something that had puzzled me

The spurts of energy
I couldn't control

The dreams of former lives,
the visions of Christ

Atlantis sinking into
ocean, centuries drowning

Was it terrible?

No, it was divine,
for I began to hear an
answer to my questions

I began to hear you
in my head

At first, there were
other voices, voices
telling me to give up

But suddenly, they went
away, and you were left

A voice that was my
voice, a spiritual connection
to God

Or whatever you are,
Self

I was in touch and I
knew my sanity

And then?

I was able to
know what I must do

I left my man, my
children and found that
I could love

The world became a
glorious place, I began
to heal

Do you understand
the risk you took by
assuming control?

I knew suddenly I could
function

Without the madness, the
anger, the fanatical
search for holiness

I became a person

Now I would like to be
human and whole

Self, what do I do?

Poet and woman,
you must know your body

Its cyclic ebb and flow
of energies

The colour of your blood
and bone, the stretch of
muscles

The effect of seasons
and weather on your brain

The dying of individual
cells and rebirth

The tenderness of a hair
pulled from the skull

The taste of your
saliva, the smell of your
faeces

And when you know this,
you must learn the
physical structures of

Trees and animals,
of flowers, insects,
reptiles and dinosaurs

The vertebrae of birds,
the anatomy of an
ape's ankle

The reaction between
sodium and a chloride

You must know the stones
of a mountain and the
stones of an ocean

And the stones of a planet
still unexplored

You must taste rainbows
and hear colours

Touch music with your
fingertips

Balance the universe
on your shoulders

Fight dragons, see ghosts,
drink hemlock

But most of all, you must
test your reality

And refuse to believe
in people's dreams

Until you too have
shared this awakening

And seen that land
so far away, unplotted
and unexamined

Until you arrive

And know, not with
the trust of a child,
but with the calm vision
of a prophet on a
mountain-top

Who can see that
earth curves forever
past the straight lines
of the heart

This would be just a
beginning

This would be the
merest speck of dust

That must gather you into
the wholeness
that you want

My instincts tell me
there are quicker ways
and more direct

To the cave of the
ancients, the scrolls
of the universe

Where all secrets
are revealed

Where all doubts
vanish into calm

And knowledge of
other people and wisdom,
which is knowledge of
your self

To know you, Self,
is my longing

For I feel strongly
that with you, the
structure of the universe
would be easy as child's
play

Am I wrong?

Poet and woman,
you are not wrong

But you are misled
to think that wisdom
stops with me

I am but an iota
of what can be learned
of life

And if life's purpose
is to acquaint us with
our natures

Then wisdom is the act
of knowing the secrets
of the universe

You cannot be separate

There is wholeness

All women are sisters

*And joy and pain are
universal*

*Flooding our every
cell and stone and flower*

*Causing us to war,
to sleep, to starve and
make love*

Self, what are you?

*I am the deity of
Gail Fox, the muse, the
guardian angel*

*The conscience, the
guide, the door into
eternity*

*I am the threshold
between the worlds*

The spirit of joy

*The bubble on the
surface of a stream*

The stone at the bottom

*I am a river, I am
an energy*

I am a haunting in my
Father's house

I am the truth as
you shall know it

I am the word, I am
the breath you take

I am Christ, the Redeemer,
I am Shiva of the many
arms, I am Buddha, I am
Moses

I am the Commandments
and the Law

I am rebirth, I am
Karma

I am the wheel of
prayer

I am grass and sky
and lightning

I am telepathy, I am
magic

I am a dowsing rod
I am a horse with wings

I am grapes in the
harvest

I am music, I am poetry

I am science, I am
alchemy

I am the Philosopher's
Stone

I am the Sphinx, and
the oracle

The Pantheon of Zeus

I am Hercules, I am
Jason

I am the Golden Fleece

I am a Titan, I am
a warrior

I am the Seven Seas

I am you, poet and
woman, if you would
understand me

Self, I find you
arrogant, or perhaps
you are speaking metaphor

In what way am I you,
if you are all?

You are me when you
listen

You are when you
let me through

Poet and woman, do you
hear me or must I
drive you mad so that
you will reconnect again?

Madmen are in touch
with self

And think because of that
they are divine

All people are divine,
poet and woman

This is the lot of the
ordinary

But the extraordinary
are those who can't believe

Who see with one eye
instead of two

And keep their energy
in chains and short
circuits like the builders
of the bomb

Hiroshima is a dream
of the extraordinary ones
whose hands cannot agree

If you are hearing,
poet and woman, you are me

Self, I hear

But find it difficult
to understand that if
I am you I am everything

How can that be possible?

When I am so
different from those
around me, so remote

Where is the difference?

In the heart or in the eye?

The eye is God's deceiver,
but the heart is the
universe, the unduplicated
truth

The heart is the brain
and the brain is the fool

My mind is ever-active,
I think and go nowhere

But fall into confusion,
anger and doubt about
my loved ones

If I trusted my heart
I would know

Is that what you are
telling me?

*If your heart is pure,
yes*

*But yours has an onion
which must be cooked
before it spoils*

How do I cook the
onion, Self, how do I
want my past to be?

*The past should be
the present*

*Should flow as a fact,
a consciousness, a
myth realized*

But I don't like my
past, I fear the anger,
the loneliness

*I do not mean that
you remember everything*

I mean that you
remember what is good

For you have been taught
by the terrible, and
the good shall influence
you all your days

Self, if that were
possible, I would rejoice

But something makes me
hesitate, back off

Poet and woman, the
mind is a tricky instrument

And knows next to nothing
about time or space

But the heart, poet
and woman, try the heart

My heart tells me
I am good and that my
anger is played out

But what is anger?

Anger is the important
means of gaining strength
for those who have no
heart

*Anger is the weapon of a
mind at war with itself*

*Anger is the badge we
wear to identify in our
confusion who we are*

But surely there are
better ways

*In the moment when we
speak, music plays,
composed in another
century*

*Yet it speaks for now,
for its language is
symbol and archetype
of the struggling soul*

*You know this music
so well you almost do
not listen*

*But I tell you, your
ears must be a child's*

So I must retain
my innocence.

*You must retain your
awareness as you grow
old*

And the familiar world
grows shadows around
your face

The young need nothing,
they are whole

But the old begin to
splinter and decay

Walls crumble, cities
fall, civilizations
drown

Because there is no
innocence left to battle

The harsh scrutiny of
the knowing eye, the
bored mouth that has
forgotten how to kiss

The unexamined dance
of death in life

Self, what is death?

Sometimes I fear not
the death of me

But of those
without whom I would
stand alone

Poet and woman,
death is the hardening
of the spirit

The cancer of the mind

Attacks of homesickness,
attacks of heartache

It is sadness, the
loss of friendship

Departures, separations,
the breaking of homes

Death of the body
is not what we fear

But the death of our
ability to feel

To wonder at memory,
at the mystery
that is in dream

Consciousness unfolding
with every blink
of the eye and beat
of the heart

Orgasm, ecstasy

What is sexuality?

I am drawn to both
men and women

And find little difference
in my needs between the
two

If that is honest,
you are fortunate

For you can choose
a person instead of
a conditioned role

That so many are forced
to play as they attempt
to grow

Sexuality is
an awareness from
childhood of what mothers
do

And how fathers leave home
to enter

A world of numbers, facts,
and distances

All measurable and
calculated by the brain

So much that is human
is lost by this stupid
division of tasks,
and love is frozen

Self, what is love?

Love is the great
heart of the universe

The life-force

The asexual sexuality
at its most potent

The physical fire,
the reaction of chemicals

The eyes wise and open
to the divinity in all
persons

The power of a great
relationship between
two people

I have known this
love, Self

Poet and woman,
if you have known this
love once in a lifetime,
you are blessed

*Most people know only
indifference*

How did love happen?

I met a person
with whom I could be
totally myself

There was nothing I
could not share
or communicate

It was a gift

That person has gone

Are you sad?

Sometimes I see this
person in another's
face

Or another's words

Or in the failure of
a relationship

But I include this
person in my present

With this beautiful
human being, I experienced
wholeness

And now?

I feel less

But the wholeness
I knew with this person

I now find in myself

Praise